STEP OUT OF THE SHADOWS

HELPING WIDOWS MOVE PAST GRIEF

8TH ANNIVERSARY EDITION
REVISED, EXPANDED & UPDATED

JEANITA JINNAH

Nayla Book Publishers
Michigan

Step Out of the Shadows
Helping Widows Move Past Grief
Copyright © 2016, 2024 by Jeanita Jinnah

Nayla Book Publishers
P.O. Box 80714
Lansing, MI 48908
naylabooks@gmail.com
info@naylabookpublishers.com
naylabookpublishers.com

All Scripture quotations are taken from the Holy Bible: New American Standard Bible (NASB) and the Holy Bible: King James Version (KJV). All rights reserved.

All rights reserved.
No part of this book may be reproduced, scanned, or distributed in any printed or electronic form without permission. Please do not participate in or encourage piracy of copyrighted materials in violation of the author's rights. Purchase only authorized editions.

Paperback ISBN: 978-0-9863889-4-1
Ebook ISBN: 978-0-9863889-5-8

To Widows Everywhere

"You have turned for me my
mourning into dancing;
you have loosed my sackcloth and
girded me with gladness."
† Psalm 30:11 †

Contents

A Note From the Author vii

Introduction xi

My Story 1

Society's Label 19

Step Out of the Shadows of Your Former Life 27

Letting Go of What Has Died 33

See Yourself Whole Again 39

Celebrate Your Former Life, But Don't Become Weighed Down By It 43

Allow God's Love to Heal You 47

Absence of A Covering 59

Your Destiny Awaits You 65

Afterword 73

A Note From The Author

I CAN'T BELIEVE it's been eight years.

When I decided to share my story of becoming a widow after the untimely death of my husband, I did not know how my story would be received.

But I felt the time was right to talk about my experience of losing a spouse at a young age, the subsequent grief and depression that followed, and my healing process.

Not only was writing this book therapeutic for me but I believed it would also help other women who are experiencing grief and depression after losing their spouse.

But what amazed me were the people, who are not widows themselves, that were also impacted by this book. People would stop me to tell me how *Step Out Of The Shadows* helped them gain a better understanding of some of the challenges and obstacles widows face after losing a spouse.

And as a result, these people felt that they were better equipped to help, and empathize, with those who are struggling through grief. They felt that they could be more supportive of them through the grieving process when they had more knowledge.

This was very encouraging to me because I can remember some very uncomfortable moments with people who would come up to me, although well-meaning, and say the wrong thing at the wrong time. I realized then that people just didn't know what to say or how to approach a grieving widow.

So, this book has been a timely blessing to both me and to those who were impacted by it.

I want to say 'Thank You!' to all who supported me throughout my journey of grief and healing, and in my decision to share my story with the world so that widows would know that they are not alone and that they are supported.

And, that no matter how dark the night, you too can rise out of the ashes of your grief and lead a productive and fulfilling life again.

To all those who grieve, may you

not get stuck in your grief. May you have the strength and the courage to step out of the shadows of the life you once lived with your spouse and step into the destiny that awaits you in your new life.

I love you and wish you all the best! ♥

Jeanita Jinnah
Author, Entrepreneur, Inventor

Introduction

ACCORDING TO THE U.S. Census Bureau nearly 1 million women are widowed each year in the United States.

At least 258 million women around the world have been widowed, and nearly one in ten of them live in devastating poverty.

Often, widows are left to care for young children alone.

Since 2001, over 7,000 U.S. service members have lost their lives in Iraq and Afghanistan. Their widows are often left to grieve alone.

The September 11, 2001 (911) terror attacks claimed the lives of 2,977 people, and left many widows and children to pick up the pieces.

Death crosses racial, cultural, and economic boundaries. Death is no respecter of persons. All the lines and the 'isms' are blurred when death comes knocking at your door.

Do you know a widow or widower? What do you need to know? First of all, acknowledge their pain. Pain is real and is expected when someone loses a loved one.

Acknowledge their grief. I know it can be uncomfortable being around a grieving person who is deep in sorrow, but grief and sadness are a normal part of life that we will all experience one day.

Give them time to heal. When you

injure yourself physically and are left with a wound or scar it takes time for the wound to heal. It doesn't heal overnight. And just like with a physical injury, an emotional wound takes time to heal. People need time to go through all the stages of grief (shock, denial, anger, bargaining, depression, acceptance, etc.). It doesn't happen overnight. Bottom line: it takes time.

What can you do to help? Offer a hug. A hug is like a smile in many ways. There's just something comforting about a loving hug. It says to someone, I care about you, I love you and I want the best for you. Sometimes a hug can say more than a thousand words. So, offer a widow a hug today.

Something else you can do is offer a helping hand. The turmoil that a family experiences following the sudden death of a loved one cannot be overstated. Suddenly, you feel like your world has been turned upside down.

Something as simple as offering to take the kids for a few hours so that mom can take a break, or dropping off a hot meal or a few bags of groceries means the world to the mom who is struggling to cope.

You might also consider paying for a weekly cleaning service to clean the family's home for a few weeks so that they don't have to worry about this while they are making funeral arrangements, and receiving friends and family and well-wishers.

Offer to mow the grass or pay for a lawn care service so that the grieving person can grieve and not have to worry about these menial tasks for a few days while they are transitioning following the death of their spouse.

Also, if you are able you might consider offering financial support or financial counseling services. Funeral expenses can be costly so helping to pay some of the funeral expenses or relocation expenses, if the family has to relocate to a new home or a new city/state, is extremely helpful.

These are just some of the ways you can help and offer support to a grieving widow. Any thoughtful acts of kindness, no matter how big or small, are a great blessing to a widow.

Finally, do not turn away. As uncomfortable as grieving, depression and death are these are just some of the ways we connect with one another on a human level. It's easy to love and support each other when things are going well. But can you be there through the difficult days and the dark nights?

Job's friends sat down with him among the ashes and mourned with him for seven days and seven nights. Then Job began to curse the day he was born and that he did not die in the womb. And his friends struggled to come up with an answer for why Job was going through the things he was going through.

Sometimes we will never be able to come up with an answer for why we have to suffer and grieve down here on earth. But what we do understand is that this is all part of living in a fallen and sinful world. But from the beginning this was not God's plan. When God created the heavens and the earth, and man, He proclaimed that everything He had created was good. The earth was sinless and man followed God's laws and obeyed Him.

But when the serpent deceived Eve in the garden to eat of the fruit of the tree which God had forbidden them to touch, and Eve in turn gave it to Adam and he did eat, in that moment a curse was brought upon man and the earth that we are still living under this day.

And just like death and grief touches all of our lives, regardless of our economic and social status in life, so too does suffering and pain touch us regardless of if we are good or evil.

We saw in the book of Job that all of Job's hardships did not come upon him because he was evil. They came upon him because he was good and pleased God, and Satan was envious of Job and of the faith and confidence God had in Job. So Satan convinced God to test Job's faith to see if he would remain faithful to God. And as God knew Job would, Job remained faithful to God through the tests even though Job's wife told him to curse God and die.

Remain faithful through the trials of life. Lean on your faith in God and believe that God will see you through.

My Story

IT'S QUITE POSSIBLE that I was the shyest girl in my school - elementary, middle school and high school. I really didn't talk to many people, never voluntarily participated in class, and mostly kept to myself. I liked it that way.

Several years ago I ran into a former classmate; she and I recognized each other immediately. As we were both reminiscing about our time in school she said that she was also really shy in school. In fact, she was so shy that her classmates voted her 'most shy girl' in school. (So I guess there actually was someone else as shy as me.)

Well, as she grew up and became an adult she said that she did not like this vote from her classmates. So she vowed as an adult not to let this designation of her by her classmates follow her into adulthood. She made it her goal to step outside of her childhood shyness and be a more outgoing adult. She said she now goes out of her way to talk to as many people as she can. She refused to let her shyness rule her life.

She and I did not share this same philosophy (lol). I embraced my shyness as part of who I am. But,

I've also learned that as an adult it's really hard to go very far in life with shyness clinging to your ankles holding you back. So I was forced to strike a balance between embracing who I am and stepping out of my shyness, when needed, to be bold and courageous in pursuing my hopes and dreams. Now I am a proud introvert who is reserved and quiet, yet strong and determined when pursuing my goals.

I grew up in the Midwest with a mom and dad who were loving but very strict and protective of their kids - especially their daughters. My parents were very religious and raised their kids with a Christian foundation under the very strict teachings of the Pentecostal church. We spent a lot of time in church with two services on Sunday, Bible Class on Wednesday and a midweek service on Thursday. We also had a weekly choir rehearsal and a daily prayer at 12:00 noon during the week. Again, we were in church a lot.

I was fine with going to church, but I think some of my siblings may have been a little resentful at times because there were other things and activities that they wanted to participate in. But it was hard because my parents were strong believers in their kids being in church whenever they were there, and they were mostly there whenever the church doors opened.

As you can imagine, I lived a very sheltered life. I spent a lot of time in my room reading and listening to music. I loved to be alone. I never participated in any after school activities and never felt like I was missing out on anything. My friends were actually in church as much as me. Such was my world.

I did attend college after high school but I went to a local University and lived at home while I was in school. I did not leave home until I met and married my husband.

Speaking of my husband, Ahmed and I met at church. He grew up in a family who were a part of the Muslim faith. Ahmed converted to Christianity when he was a young man, as did several of his siblings.

Ahmed and I never really talked at church, other than a casual greeting of "Praise the Lord," which is how we greeted everyone in our church. After we were married, he would joke that he had tried to speak to me a few times but I had brushed him off. He actually said he thought I was stuck-up at the time. Which is funny to me because I wasn't stuck-up I was just painfully shy. I wouldn't talk to too many people unless I knew them or felt comfortable around them. I was always guarded.

Our courtship and subsequent marriage was really God ordained as I never looked at him in that way, and as I said before we never talked. But I believe that God was behind the scenes orchestrating things so that

I would one day marry an amazing man and become his life partner as we journeyed through life together.

I won't bore you with all the details but Ahmed and I did eventually get married, after a brief courtship, and moved about 400 miles away from both of our families. (I was 24 years old.) We were in love and very happy together. We went about building our life together and as far as we saw it were prepared to spend the rest of our lives together.

In many ways Ahmed and I were alike - we had the same values, were strong in our faith, and were committed to loving each other and always being there for one another. But we were also different in that

Ahmed was outgoing and loved being around people. And I was quiet and reserved and loved being alone with my thoughts; and I enjoyed my peace and quiet. But we somehow made it work and it worked out fine.

For our fourth wedding anniversary Ahmed and I decided to purchase anniversary rings as gifts for each other. But when we told people about this some were not hesitant to voice their disapproval, because according to them there was an established wedding anniversary milestone gifts guide in place that couples use as a guide when giving wedding anniversary gifts. Therefore, they thought that purchasing anniversary rings was something that should have been done for a 10th anniversary, not a fourth anniversary.

Ahmed and I just dismissed these people and their disapproval and kept on living our lives, the way we wanted to live it. Not according to someone else's ideas of how we should live our lives. People are funny sometimes.

But looking back on it I'm glad that we decided to celebrate our fourth wedding anniversary the way we did because little did we know that when our fifth wedding anniversary came around we would receive some devastating news.

Ahmed received news from his doctor, shortly before our fifth wedding anniversary, that he had a cancerous tumor in his brain, and it was inoperable. This news hit us like a runaway freight train running full speed off the tracks. Neither of us was ready for this. This news caught us completely off guard. Why was this happening to us? And what did this mean for us going forward?

Going forward, what this meant for us was a putting on hold of all of our plans and having to now juggle doctor appointments, chemotherapy and radiation treatments, hospital stays and the side effects of the cancer and all of the treatments. The doctor told us early on that his cancer was inoperable so he was focused on treating Ahmed's cancer the best way he could and keeping him comfortable.

Ahmed took his cancer diagnosis in stride and immediately started believing in God for a miracle, in spite of what the doctors said. It was hard for me to watch my strong athletic husband go through this battle with the beast that is cancer. And over time the cancer started to affect him and he began to weaken physically as a result. But he still had faith in God, and I would do nothing or say nothing to shake his faith.

If only the doctors prescribed to this same plan, too. We were at his oncologist's office one day when suddenly, out of nowhere, the doctor blurted out that the cancer has progressed "and will probably take your life in six months." This outburst from the doctor caught both of us by surprise. Ahmed was so upset with his doctor for being so blatantly bold and heartless with his words. It really rattled him. Ahmed said to me afterwards that no one but God really knows how much time we have here on earth. He pointed out that the doctor, who happened to be overweight, could go to bed one night and never wake up. So how could he tell Ahmed that he would be dead in six months?

Well, these words affected Ahmed more than I even realized at the time. It rattled his faith and he was never able to recover from the prognosis the doctor had so heartlessly spoken over him.

My thoughts on this are that there

are some people who want to know this type of information and will ask the doctor how long he thought they had to live, and become resigned to it and start making plans for their death. But then there are other people who, no matter how impossible the situation looks, still have faith in God for a miracle because miracles happen everyday, and miracles come from God, not man.

I think that doctors should know what type of patient they are dealing with and adjust their bedside manners accordingly. Because I do not think that it's right for any doctor to heartlessly strip a patient of the last hope he is clinging to - his faith in God for healing. This doctor was rude and insensitive and so callously ripped the faith away from my husband and he was never able to recover from it.

Well the cancer did not take his life in six months. He actually lived for another year and a half before succumbing to the cancer. But his faith was never the same.

After my husband died I was devastated. As I sat next to his hospital bed, after watching him take his last breath, my exact words were "what am I supposed to do now?" I was 31 years old and I had just watched my future die in a cold hospital room from a vicious disease. This wasn't supposed to happen to me; to us. But here I was uncertain of my future without my sweet husband.

We buried Ahmed on a cold December day surrounded by friends and family. My life would never be the same. I told you earlier that I lived at home with my parents until I got married. I always say that I moved from my parents' home to my husband's home. I had never lived on my own before. But now that Ahmed was gone I was on my own for the first time.

I had lived such a sheltered life. When I lived with my parents they took care of everything. And when I lived with my husband he took care of everything for us. For the first time in my life I had to learn how to take care of things for myself. This was all unfamiliar and scary for me.

Taking care of a home, paying the bills, mowing the lawn, being responsible for home and car repairs; essentially making my own decisions by myself for the first time in my life. I felt completely overwhelmed by it all.

But here I was, on my own, trying to navigate through life and the subsequent grief and depression that followed the death of my husband. Life felt so unfair. I didn't understand why God would allow this to happen to me. Not to mention that now that I was a widow the world would never look at me the same again.

LIFE seems so UNFAIR at times.
You expect to go left
and life takes you right.
You expect to be UP
but somehow you keep FALLING
DOWN. Why don't you just make up
your mind, LIFE?

Pure and undefiled religion in the sight of our God and Father is this: to visit orphans and widows in their distress, and to keep oneself unstained by the world.
† (James 1:27) †

Society's Label

I WANT TO take a few moments to encourage those of you who are widowed to begin to step out of the shadows of your widowhood.

As a widow myself, I know that society can place a stigma, or label, on widows. You walk around feeling branded, and often ashamed. Not to mention the lack of compassion and empathy you feel around you. If this is you, then this message is for you!

I want to encourage you to step out of the shadows. The shadow of the label society places on you, and the shadow of the life you used to lead with your spouse.

Widows are often a forgotten class in society. More focus gets placed on those who are married or single. If you are married or single you always have a place to belong. You are sure to find social events, conferences, and gatherings geared toward both married couples and singles. Rarely are there any such events for widows.

Newly widowed women can quickly find themselves being slowly edged out of the social circles they were once a part of, along with their spouse.

Eventually, these newly widowed

women begin to sense a climate change towards them, by their married friends, as they try and continue to be active in these groups after the loss of their husband.

This coolness usually comes from the other women in the group, who, for whatever reason, no longer see the widow in the same light. She is now looked upon as a threat to have around, and no longer made to feel welcomed in the group. An unattached woman is sadly sometimes perceived as a threat by a married woman, so she prefers to keep her at a safe distance, and hence away from her husband.

This can be devastating for someone who has just suffered the loss of her spouse because what she needs now more than anything is the loving support of friends and family, and to feel some sense of normalcy during this dark and difficult time. But her sudden status change in life has left her without the support system she desperately needs.

And society now forces the newly widowed woman to change her marital status from married to single, against her will.

Why? Because whenever you are required to fill out applications or complete any type of paperwork, where it asks for your marital status, the options on the form are usually "married," or "single."

There is rarely an option for "widowed" on the form. This is when a widow has to take a few moments to ponder before answering the question. Am I still married, or am I now single? To me a single person is one who has never been married; but on the other hand, since you have no living spouse, can you legitimately answer the question — married?

This is a difficult choice to suddenly have forced upon you. By lumping everyone together with the "single" group you are in essence negating everything that person has been through. Is it really that hard to place an option for "widowed" on the form? This would help to solve this awkward dilemma.

It's been my experience that these societal labels can sometimes carry over into the church as well, as the church also puts its focus and resources more toward married couples and singles, while ignoring the widows.

Hopefully this will start to change. Perhaps one day the church will also be a welcoming environment for widows so that we no longer have to hold our heads down in shame, and be made to feel like outcasts who have to bear the weight of our loss alone.

The church should be a place where we can go to find healing for not just our bodies, but also for our souls. It's time for the church to start paying attention to its widows, giving them the love and the support they need, while also giving them the time they need to heal.

Cast your burden upon the Lord and
He will sustain you;
He will never allow the righteous to
be shaken.
† (Psalm 55:22) †

Step Out of the Shadows of Your Former Life

NOW THAT YOUR spouse is no longer living, you have to begin to pick up the pieces of your shattered life and start moving forward and carving out a new life for yourself.

If you are newly widowed and the pain of your loss is still fresh, you need to focus right now on going through the healing process — and it is a process. It takes time. Don't allow anyone to rush you through this process; take all the time you need to heal, then make a concerted effort to move forward with your life.

We can never bring back our spouse, nor can we go back and re-create the life we once shared with him. As difficult as it is to have to start all over again, we must be willing to start afresh, and learn to make the most of our new life without our spouse.

I've always heard the saying, time heals all wounds. I don't know how true this is, but time certainly does help to ease the pain. In time you will be able to breathe again, smile again, enjoy a beautiful sunset again, and feel alive again. It's natural to want to carry on with the life you once shared with your spouse, but it's no longer possible, or even healthy.

As Christians, when we marry,

the Bible encourages us to become one — "the two shall become one." One in unity, love, and commitment. We can no longer lead a separate life apart from our spouse; we must begin to merge our lives together so that the two become one. When this happens, you become like a two-strand cord, which, when it is braided together and becomes intertwined, becomes stronger and harder to break apart.

But once a spouse dies, this two-strand cord must be broken apart and once again become one. This is not easy to do as by now all of the fibers of the cords have begun to blend together, making it virtually impossible to tear apart.

This is why grief is so difficult. You're

still holding on and clinging to a part of you that has died. It is, therefore, not easy for you to complete the separation. But you must, because you have to now move forward as an individual person again.

So, how do you begin to step out of the shadows of your former life? By giving yourself permission to let go of that part of you that has died. By beginning to see yourself as a whole person again without your spouse. By celebrating the life you had with your spouse without being weighed down by it, unable to move forward. And by allowing God's love and compassion for you to heal and make you whole again.

"I can do all things through Christ who strengthens me" (Philippians

4:13).

God has great love and compassion for the widow, and the orphan — those who are without a covering, and henceforth the most vulnerable in society. He said He would be their covering, protector, and provider. He will help them when they feel weak, and protect them when they are defenseless.

God's hand is extended to you. Grab hold of His hand and allow Him to assist you with your first few wobbly steps until your feet and ankle bones are strengthened enough, and you are able to walk on your own. Step out of the shadows, and into your destiny.

Letting Go of What Has Died

IT IS NEVER easy to lose a spouse or loved one. Even though death is a normal part of life, it still doesn't seem natural to me. To know that you will never again enjoy your loved one's presence here on earth can be difficult to accept in the beginning.

To know that you will never be able to hear his voice again, to hear his laugh again, or to share your secret thoughts with him isn't an easy reality to embrace.

I remember shortly after Ahmed died, there were times when I would see something interesting or hear something funny and for a quick second I would go to turn to him to ask him if he saw that. I caught myself doing this a few times but was quickly reminded that he wasn't there and that he would never be there again for me to share these moments with. This is when the reality of his death began to sink in. Death is like that bitter pill that even though you don't want to, you know you must swallow it.

But in order to move forward you must give yourself permission to let go of the part of you that has died.

Grief is a normal part of the healing process after the loss of a spouse. But never being able to rise above that grief and be happy again is not normal. You should not be content with wearing your mourning garments the rest of your life. At some point you must take off your mourning garments and commence to living life again.

This doesn't mean that you forget about your spouse or that you never again feel the weight of his absence. Your spouse will always be a part of you. But your grief shouldn't cause you to shut yourself up in the casket with him, burying all of your hopes and dreams, and your will to live and face another day. Your spouse would not want you to die along with him. He would want you to live. And he would want you to live well.

Letting go doesn't mean forgetting. It just means letting go of all the hurt and the pain associated with death, while embracing the love and joy you shared with your spouse when he was alive.

Remember the good times. Let these memories comfort and nourish you. Don't focus on his death. Instead, celebrate the impact his life had on you, and on the world.

MISS ME but let me go,
for this is a journey we all
must take and each must go alone.
It's all part
of the MASTER'S PLAN,
a step on the road to Home.
-Unknown

He heals the brokenhearted
And binds up their wounds.
† Psalm 147:3 †

See Yourself Whole Again

PRIOR TO MEETING and marrying your spouse, you probably never thought of yourself as incomplete. In your youthful exuberance, you were probably focused on pursuing your dreams and conquering the world. And you probably felt like you could do anything you set your mind to.

This doesn't have to change after the death of a loved one. You can be strong again, whole again, even after losing a spouse. And this should be your goal. It's really all in your belief system. If you can see it and believe it, you can have it, be it, and achieve it.

How do you see your life? Do you see a life where you barely drag yourself out of bed each morning, willing yourself to place one foot in front of the other, and forcing yourself to make it through yet another miserable day? Or, do you see yourself rising above the pain and the grief, looking forward with hopeful expectation to a better tomorrow, a happier tomorrow, and a life once again filled with joy?

Start to see yourself whole again. Believe that it is possible, and do whatever is necessary to make it happen.

God wants each of us to be happy and live an abundant life. He knows that we will occasionally go through tests and trials, and the things that come to try our faith. God never promised us that we wouldn't experience these things. But He did promise that He would always be with us, no matter what.

When the pain of my loss was still fresh I couldn't even see past the grief, but deep down inside I somehow knew that I would make it through, because I knew God would help me through.

I also gave myself permission to grieve. I would occasionally remind myself, "it's okay to be here, but you can't stay here long." I knew that if I stayed in a perpetual state of grief the rest of my life I would eventually die in my grief. So I reminded myself that although what I was experiencing was normal, I couldn't get stuck in it.

Don't allow yourself to get stuck in grief. Press your way through it. God is there to help you through the process.

Celebrate Your Former Life, But Don't Become Weighed Down By It

PEOPLE CHOOSE TO honor their deceased loved ones in various ways. Some set up scholarship funds in the name of their loved ones. Others establish non-profit foundations to continue their loved one's legacy, while helping others. And some plant trees in honor of their loved ones.

However you decide to honor your loved one — big or small — this helps to keep their memory alive, and at the same time gives you a positive focus to direct your energy. Celebrate your loved one's life instead of focusing on their death. Use this painful event to bring about good and a positive change to the world, in their honor.

My husband's memory is alive in my heart. I dedicated my first book to him. He will always be remembered. He brought so much happiness to my life. He was my biggest supporter, and just an overall good guy. I will always carry the love and the nuggets of wisdom he left with me.

When I come up against something that I feel is too difficult to accomplish I remember what Ahmed used to always tell me — "It's not about strength, it's know-how." In other words, you may not have the physical strength to do something, but you can find other ways to accomplish a task just by using your brain.

And you know what? He was right! I've put this nugget of truth to work in my life and have been able to solve difficult problems by using my brain to come up with alternative ways of accomplishing difficult tasks when I didn't necessarily have the physical strength to do it. Brute force is good, but what happens when your strength begins to wane? Then you are forced to use the strongest muscle you possess - your brain. What a wonderful gift my husband has left with me. I shall always cherish him.

Learn to do good;
Seek justice,
Reprove the ruthless,
Defend the orphan,
Plead for the widow.
† (Isaiah 1:17) †

Allow God's Love to Heal You

I'VE DISCOVERED GOD'S love through pain and loss. And I've discovered that God's love heals.

We're all accustomed to going to the doctor in search of a magic pill that can cure all of our ills, and take away all of our aches and pains. We are convinced that the doctor can help us with a magic drug. But usually the doctor's treatments only offer us a temporary relief, and we find ourselves having to go back to the doctor over and over again to receive more of these "treatments." It doesn't heal us, it only creates a cycle of dependency - in my opinion. (I'm sure the doctor is happy about this.) We must eventually get to the root cause of the problem, and then find a way to eliminate the problem at its root so that our symptoms are removed.

God's love has medicinal properties, and can do what no other power can do. His love can mend the broken heart, give sight to the blind, cause the lame to walk, and the mute to speak. His love heals us and makes us whole.

When my grief was still raw, and I found myself barely able to drag myself out of bed in the morning, it was hard for me to see past my grief.

My world was encapsulated by grief.

At the time, I had a purple chair in my living room that faced a big window. I would sit for hours in this chair, staring out the window. I would find myself sitting there watching the sun come up and then watching it go back down again.

I would only leave my purple chair to go into the kitchen to fix myself something to eat, to go to the bathroom, to drag myself to bed, or to reluctantly go to work. Other than that I really didn't have the energy to do much of anything. The weight of my grief kept me glued to this purple chair. My whole world was dark and cloudy. I felt all alone.

During this period of grief, there were times when I would walk into the bathroom, and as I passed by the bathroom mirror I would stop and do a double take at my reflection in the mirror. I noticed that there appeared to be a glow around my face, and it was noticeable. I would stand there for a moment looking at myself in the mirror, thinking to myself, it must be the make-up. But then there were times when this glow would appear on my face when I wasn't wearing any make-up. So I knew it couldn't have been the make-up.

Around this time, I can remember being at church one Sunday morning, and one of the church mothers coming up to me after church asking me to please forgive her for staring at me during the service. She said that as she sat in the front of the church, near the pulpit area, she saw what appeared to be a glow around me, and she couldn't stop staring at me. I told her that I did not notice her staring at all.

And then there was another time at church, after Bible class was over, when someone else came up to me and asked me what I was doing to my skin because it was almost radiant. I told her that I wasn't doing anything new or different to my skin. I really did not know what she was talking about at the time.

Approximately a year and a half into my husband's battle with cancer he contracted shingles; possibly as a result of the stress of his illness or the chemotherapy treatments he was receiving. I had read that shingles are a form of the chickenpox virus, and like chickenpox, are highly contagious.

As a kid I never had chickenpox so I was aware of the risk factors involved of me potentially catching this virus. And, as luck would have it, exactly two weeks after my husband contracted shingles, I contracted chickenpox.

As an adult, this virus was rough on me and had me confined to my bed for a couple of weeks. And being the primary caretaker for a sick spouse, this made things even more stressful for us because Ahmed and I had no family near us at the time to help out and pick up the slack; so it was just him and I. I was still trying to take care of my sick husband, but there wasn't much I could do because this virus kept me confined to my bed. At times Ahmed and I found ourselves switching roles with him trying to care for me while I myself was sick with chickenpox.

On a particular night I can remember getting up in the middle of the night to apply some itch cream. The last thing I remembered was standing in front of the bathroom mirror. Then, I must have passed out.

There was a heating vent on the floor in the bathroom and I had a very faint recollection of hitting the back of my head on this vent as I fell to the floor. I have no idea how long I was out, but what was amazing to me is what happened next.

I remember coming to as I was being lifted up off the bathroom floor.

Naturally, after passing out you would think that you would wake up to find yourself on the bathroom floor and wonder how you got there. But this did not happen to me. I came to while I was being lifted up off the floor. Ahmed was asleep the whole time. He never woke up. In fact, after I came to, I went to wake him and tell him that I think I just passed out.

A few years after this incident, once the fog had lifted on my grief, and I was now able to look back on this time with a clear head, I remembered these incidents: the passing out in the bathroom, and the standing in front of the mirror trying to figure out why my face appeared to be glowing. It suddenly hit me, and I remember saying to God, "It was you, wasn't it?!" "You were there with me that night in the bathroom, and it was you who lifted me up off the bathroom floor!" And, "You were there with me during my grief, causing your light to shine through the darkness!"

I didn't realize it at the time because the grief was so heavy, but I do understand now that God was with me the whole time. Even though at the time I felt so alone. God was there comforting me, allowing me to cry on His shoulder, and carrying me through. He tells us in His word, "I will never leave you or forsake you." I am a witness to this.

People sometimes desert you. It's not always comfortable being around a grieving person because you may not know what to say to comfort them. And let's face it, grief isn't pretty. But

God will always be with you no matter what. And He was there with me the whole time while I was in my pit of grief and despair, even though I didn't recognize it at the time.

It was God's love that brought me through. He healed my broken heart, set me back up on my feet, and gave me joy. He put a smile in my heart again. His love did what no other power could do.

God also wants to heal your broken heart. He wants to help you through the pain and the grief. He wants to be that shining light that cuts through the darkness.

God will never leave you or forsake you. He will always be with you, no matter what. You are not alone. Allow God to comfort you and strengthen you. You shall live and not die. And you will one day be able to smile again, and experience joy again. Just continue to hold onto God's loving hand. He will bring you through. Allow His love to heal you.

He will cover you with His pinions,
And under His wings you may seek refuge;
His faithfulness is a shield and bulwark.
† (Psalm 91:4) †

Absence of A Covering

OUR HUSBAND IS usually our covering, our protector, and our support. Women need the physical covering that a man brings, not because we are weak, but because we are vulnerable. It's a sad fact, but in our society women are often preyed upon and therefore vulnerable.

When people see that there is no man in a woman's life, some will try and take advantage of her. Because these people are convinced that an unprotected woman is an easy target and, therefore, have no fear of a husband ever stepping in and coming to his wife's defense.

A father is usually the first covering in a girl's life. A good father will stop at nothing to protect and shield his daughter from outside forces. He is that barrier between his little girl and the world. This father understands that there are predators out there looking for an opportunity to harm little girls, and he wants to keep his daughter safe.

A good father also wants to shield his little girl from harm. If she falls down and skins her knee, he is there to pick her up. He is there to wipe away her tears, and to make her feel safe in his arms. This daughter knows that nothing can harm her as long as her father is there.

Many of today's modern women are offended at the thought of having a man as a covering. They feel that this is a sign of weakness, as they strongly believe that a woman can, and should, do anything a man can do. And for this reason, many women will reject this God-given role of a man to cover them, and choose to step into this role themselves.

As women, we have so much on our shoulders already and, therefore, should eagerly embrace the gift that God has given to us of a godly man to be our covering. God created the man for this role, and set him over the family, and gave him the tools needed to carry out this role. And in the absence of a husband or a father to provide a covering for a woman, God steps in and fulfills this role

Himself.

God has great love for the widow and the orphan - those who are often alone and vulnerable in our society. God tells us that we should protect and defend these people from their oppressors.

We should never seek to take advantage of the widow or the orphan or to harm them in any way. Because if we do, and these poor widows or orphans cry out to God, He will surely hear them and his wrath will be stirred up, and He will kill with the sword all those who have oppressed these people; and *their* wives shall be widowed and *their* children fatherless (Exodus 22:22-24). God will surely protect widows from their oppressors.

Thus, we have nothing to fear.

With God on our side, He is more than the world against us. Therefore, we don't have to walk around with our heads hung down. We are not alone or forgotten. Even when we don't realize it, God is working behind the scenes for us, protecting us, shielding us from harm, and coming to our defense. If we cry out to Him, He hears us and comes running to our defense. We are never defenseless with God as our covering.

So in the absence of a husband to cover you, know that you have a loving Father in heaven who is ready to stand in as a covering for you. Receive God's love and His protection today.

Your Destiny Awaits You

SO YOU'VE GONE through the worst, and you have survived. You are stronger than you thought you were. Life has a way of catching you by surprise and throwing you for a loop. But even though you never saw it coming you were able to adjust to it and move on. Yes, it may have caught you off guard in the beginning, but something inside of you wouldn't let it destroy you.

We were all uniquely designed by God to shake off difficulties and hardships, and to rise above them. And with God as our support, and His ability to give us strength when we feel weak, we know that nothing the enemy throws at us can harm us. Satan's fiery darts cannot penetrate us as long as God is on our side. If we can learn to keep our eyes on God, instead of becoming overwhelmed by the situation, we can, with God's help, make it through anything.

So take joy in knowing that once you've survived the worst that the night has to offer, joy comes in the morning. But to make it to the other side where joy abounds, you must persevere through the dark nights, knowing and believing that once you make it through, you will be rewarded on the other side.

God has a plan for your life. He's given you a hope and a bright future. Embrace the plan that God has for you. His plan is always good.

You probably never imagined life without your spouse. How could any of us have known when we stood before man and God and professed that we were in it "till death do we part" that we would actually have to one day live this out?

Still, we always expect to grow old and gray with our spouse. We expect to one day celebrate our 50th wedding anniversary surrounded by friends and loved ones. Sadly, this isn't the case for everyone, as you well know. Yet, you were blessed to have had your spouse as long as you did. That should bring some comfort to your soul.

Your husband was in your life, however brief, and you were enriched by his love and comfort for the short time that you had it. But now it is time to move on. Now it is time to accept the fact that your husband is gone and he is never coming back. Now it is time to look forward to the future with expectancy in your heart.

It is possible to have a bright future again. Step out of the chains of grief that have held you bound, and free yourself of the burden of having to grieve for your husband the rest of your life. The amount of time you grieve does not equate to the depth of the love you had for your spouse.

Free yourself of the grieving process, and allow yourself the opportunity to breathe again, to laugh again, to experience joy again. I'm not talking about another relationship. People tend to think that the only way you can move forward and be happy again is if you are in another relationship. Sometimes it's good to take a break from relationships and learn to be whole as an individual person again. There is absolutely nothing wrong with this. Love yourself and your individual uniqueness. Take this time to do some of the things you've always wanted to do but for whatever reason you never had the time to do. Give yourself permission to experience life again. You deserve it.

Your destiny is wrapped up in your attitude. The magnitude of the joy you are able to experience again will be determined by your attitude. So it helps to have an attitude of hopeful expectancy, looking forward to and expecting the best that life has to offer.

Begin to see yourself happy again, whole again, and see yourself healthy and well. Embrace your future. And remember, there is no need to be afraid because God is right there with you.

"We thank you Heavenly Father for the comfort you have offered to us during this difficult time in our lives. You have surrounded us with your love and your presence is always near. You are a Father to the fatherless and a husband to those who have no husband. You provide grace and strength when we feel

weak. You extend your hand and lift us up when we fall down. You set us back up on our feet and wipe away our tears. You are the mender of broken hearts. You've planted your love in our hearts and because of this we now have a hope and a future. You will never leave our side, you will always be there. We thank you for being our covering and our protector. Your grace is sufficient for all of our needs. Amen."

Afterword

IF YOU (or someone you know) are a widow I pray that this message brings you comfort. It is possible to rise from the ashes after losing a loved one. There is always hope for a brighter tomorrow as long as God is guiding your footsteps.

Step out of the shadows. Step into God's light. Allow the brightness of His glory to overshadow you and make you whole again. God wants to mend the broken pieces of your life. Allow Him to do it. He loves you very much. And so do I.

Healing Scriptures

God is our refuge and strength,
a very present help in trouble.
Therefore we will not fear, though
the earth should change
and though the mountains slip into
the heart of the sea.
† Psalm 46:1-2 †

Blessed be the Lord, who daily
bears our burden,
the God who is our salvation. Selah.
† Psalm 68:19 †

The righteous man will flourish like
the palm tree,
he will grow like a cedar in Lebanon.
Planted in the house of the Lord,

they will flourish in the courts of our God.
They will still yield fruit in old age;
they shall be full of sap and very green,
to declare that the Lord is upright;
He is my rock, and there is no unrighteousness in Him.
† Psalm 92:12-15 †

Bless the Lord, O my soul,
and all that is within me, bless His holy name.
Bless the Lord, O my soul,
and forget none of His benefits;
who pardons all your iniquities,
who heals all your diseases;
who redeems your life from the pit,
who crowns you with lovingkindness and compassion.
† Psalm 103-1-4 †

My heart is steadfast, O God;
I will sing, I will sing praises, even with my soul.
Awake, harp and lyre;
I will awaken the dawn!
I will give thanks to You, O Lord, among the peoples,
and I will sing praises to You among the nations.
For Your lovingkindness is great above the heavens,
and Your truth reaches to the skies.
† Psalm 108:1-4 †

The sound of joyful shouting and salvation is in the tents of the righteous;
the right hand of the Lord does valiantly.
The right hand of the Lord is exalted;
the right hand of the Lord does valiantly.
I will not die, but live,
and tell of the works of the Lord.

† Psalm 118:15-17 †

Behold, God is my salvation,
I will trust and not be afraid;
for the Lord God is my strength and song,
and He has become my salvation.
Therefore you will joyously draw water
from the springs of salvation.
† Isaiah 12:2-3 †

For You have been a defense for the helpless,
a defense for the needy in his distress,
a refuge from the storm, a shade from the heat.
† Isaiah 25:4 †

Surely our griefs He Himself bore,

and our sorrows He carried;
yet we ourselves esteemed Him stricken,
smitten of God, and afflicted.
But He was pierced through for our transgressions,
He was crushed for our iniquities;
the chastening for our well-being fell upon Him,
and by His scourging we are healed.
† Isaiah 53:4-5 †

Nayla Book Publishers

More from Jeanita:

An Open Letter to the Church:
On Faith, Holiness, and Being
Full of the Holy Ghost

The Purpose of Man

Step Out of the Shadows:
Helping Widows Move Past Grief

Website:
naylabookpublishers.com

Contact:
info@naylabookpublishers.com

www.ingramcontent.com/pod-product-compliance
Lightning Source LLC
Chambersburg PA
CBHW020700300426
44112CB00007B/461